READY, SET, DRAW!

DOGS
YOU CAN DRAW

Nicole Brecke
Patricia M. Stockland

Millbrook Press / Minneapolis

The photographs in this book are used with permission of: iStock Photo, 4, 5, 7, 19, 27; Dzianis Miraniuk/iStock Photo, 4; JR Trice/iStock Photo, 5; Boris Yankov/iStock Photo, 5; Andreas Geiser/iStock Photo, 9; Maciej Korzekwa/iStock Photo, 11; Mark Rasmussen/Fotolia, 15; Christopher O. Driscoll/iStock Photo, 23; Arthur Kwiatkowski/iStock Photo, 31.

Front cover: © iStockphoto.com; © iStockphoto.com/blackred; © Mark Rasmussen/Fotolia.com.

Edited by Melissa Johnson, Mari Kesselring
Research by Emily Temple

Text and illustrations copyright © 2010 by Lerner Publishing Group, Inc.

Millbrook Press
A division of Lerner Publishing Group, Inc.
241 First Avenue North
Minneapolis, MN 55401 U.S.A.

Website address: www.lernerbooks.com

Library of Congress Cataloging-in-Publication Data

Brecke, Nicole.
　　Dogs you can draw / by Nicole Brecke and Patricia M. Stockland.
　　　　　p.　cm. — (Ready, set, draw!)
　　　Includes index.
　　　ISBN: 978-0-7613-4159-8 (lib. bdg. : alk. paper)
　　　1. Dogs in art—Juvenile literature. 2. Drawing—Technique—Juvenile literature. I. Stockland, Patricia M. II. Title. III. Title: Dogs.
　　NC783.8.D64B74 2010
　　743.6'9772—dc22
　　　　　　　　　　　　　　　　　　　　　　　　　　　　　　　　2008036622

Manufactured in the United States of America
1 2 3 4 5 6 – BP – 15 14 13 12 11 10

TABLE OF CONTENTS

ABOUT THIS BOOK

Dogs make great friends. And they're fun subjects to draw! With the help of this book, you can start sketching your favorite furry friend. Draw a long, low, lean dachshund. Or color a tall, curly-haired, supersmart poodle. You'll soon know how to draw many different dogs.

Follow these steps to create each dog. Each drawing begins with a basic form. The form is made up of a line and a couple of shapes. These lines and shapes will help you make your drawing the correct size.

A First, read all the steps and look at the pictures. Then use a pencil to lightly draw the line and shapes shown in RED. You will erase these lines later.

B Next, draw the lines shown in BLUE.

C Keep going! Once you have completed a step, the color of the line changes to BLACK. Follow the BLUE line until you're done.

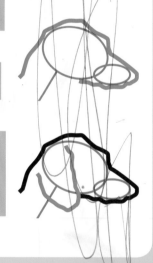

WHAT YOU WILL NEED

PENCIL SHARPENER

COLORED PENCILS

HELPFUL HINTS

Use your imagination. Be creative. If you love a certain breed of dog, read about it and then follow the steps and the pictures to create your own doggone good masterpiece.

Practice drawing different lines and shapes. All of your drawings will start with these.

ERASER

Use very light pencil lines when you are drawing.

Look for tips that will offer you good ideas on making the most of your sketch.

PENCIL

Colors are exciting. Try to use a variety of shades. This will add value, or depth, to your finished drawings.

PAPER

Keep practicing, and have fun!

HOW TO DRAW A DACHSHUND

Want a dog that's close to the ground? How about a dachshund? These protective pups are perfect for smaller places. They can be standard, miniature, or toy sized. Dachshunds were originally long, lean hunting machines, bred to track badgers. Now, these vocal dogs make great companions. Dachshunds can be all colors of red, brown, black, and tan. They can also be brindled (mixtures of black and another color) or dappled (spotted), depending on the type. Dachshunds can be smooth-, long-, or wire-haired.

1 Draw a light base oval. Then add a smaller oval and a short center line. Draw around the ovals to make the head and muzzle. Add an ear.

2 Add a large base oval at the end of the center line. Draw around this long, narrow oval for the back and the front of the main body.

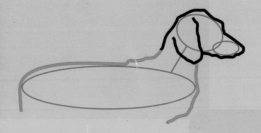

3

Make a short front leg. Draw the belly and back leg. Add a long, skinny tail and two more legs.

4 Erase your baseline and shapes.

5

Draw a circle for the eye and a half circle for the nose.

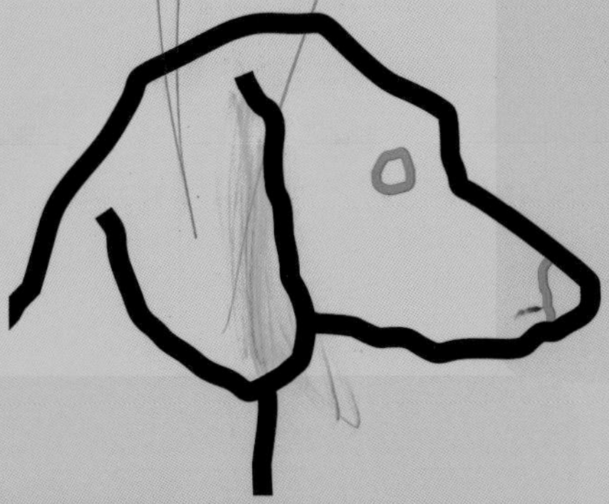

6 Now it is time to color your dachshund!

HOW TO DRAW A POODLE

Poodles are popular pups! Lots of people own poodles. These dogs have diverse looks and personalities. And they may be the smartest of all breeds. Make sure your poodle gets brain exercise in addition to long walks and fun games. This curly-haired breed can come in many different colors and different sizes, including standard, miniature, and toy. A poodle's curly coat needs lots of grooming. But unlike most long-haired dogs, it rarely sheds. Poodles make happy, energetic pets.

1 Use light lines to draw a small base circle and a large base oval. Connect them with a curved center line. Add a tail line and a small circle. Add two small ovals to the top circle. Outline the ear, head, muzzle, and neck.

Make a back line parallel to the center line, and outline the tail. Add a puffy U shape for the front leg. Draw a smaller front leg and belly. Add two long, puffy U shapes for the back legs.

3 Carefully erase your baseline and shapes. Add a small dot for an eye and a half circle for the nose.

4 Now it is time to color your poodle!

9

HOW TO DRAW A GERMAN SHEPHERD

German shepherds used to work as sheep-herding dogs in Germany. Now, German shepherds help disabled people, act as rescue dogs, work with police officers and detectives, and even star in movies. These medium-large dogs are usually black and tan. They are smart, fearless, and very active. German shepherds are also loyal and protective. They use their strong herding instincts to keep people from danger. Be ready to play if you want one of these intelligent pets. German shepherds need plenty of exercise.

1 Make a tall base oval and put a curved center line through it. Add a square to the top, with a small triangle on each of the top corners.

2 Draw around the square, triangles, and oval to make the head, ears, back, tail, and leg.

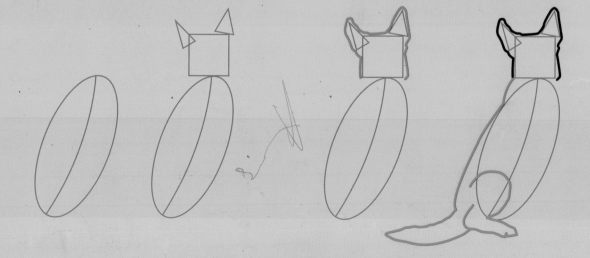

3

Draw the chest along the front of the base oval. Add four vertical lines for the front legs and paws. Add a back leg to the bottom of the oval.

4

Carefully erase your baseline and shapes. Draw a U shape for the muzzle. Add two small circles for eyes. Add a small oval with two dots for the nose.

5 Now it is time to color your German shepherd!

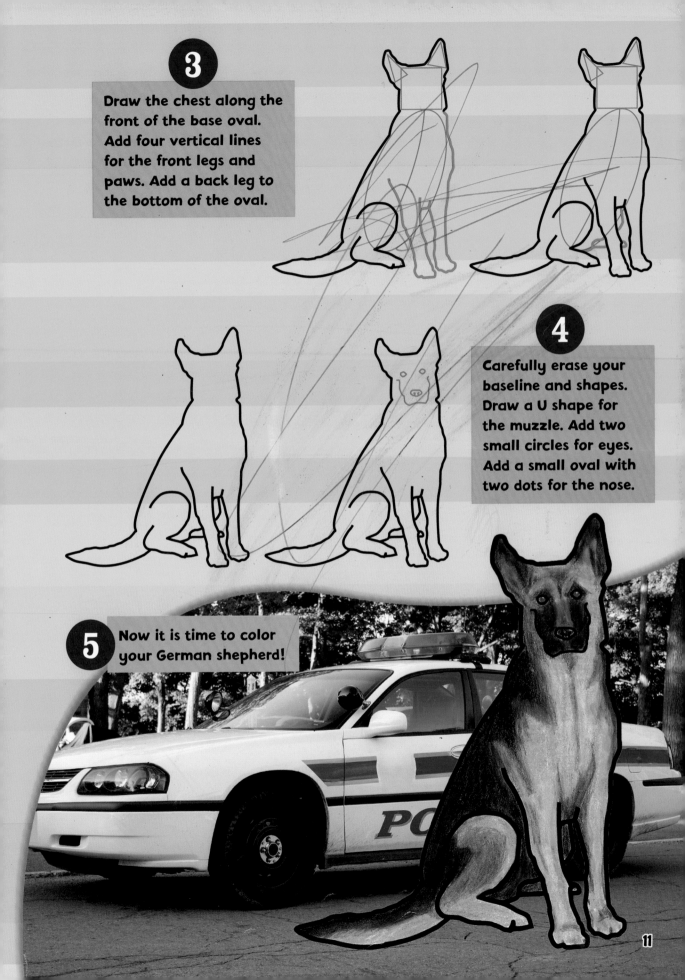

HOW TO DRAW A BOXER

Boxers are fast and graceful, using their front paws to punch and jab when playing. This friendly breed loves to have fun. Boxers were originally hunting dogs. They helped their masters hunt bison, bears, and wild boars in Germany. That's where this breed developed. A history of hunting has also made this breed loyal and protective. Boxers are usually either tan or brindle colored. Some boxers can be all or mostly white. Others have black or white markings.

1 Lightly draw two overlapping base circles. Add a curved center line and a larger circle.

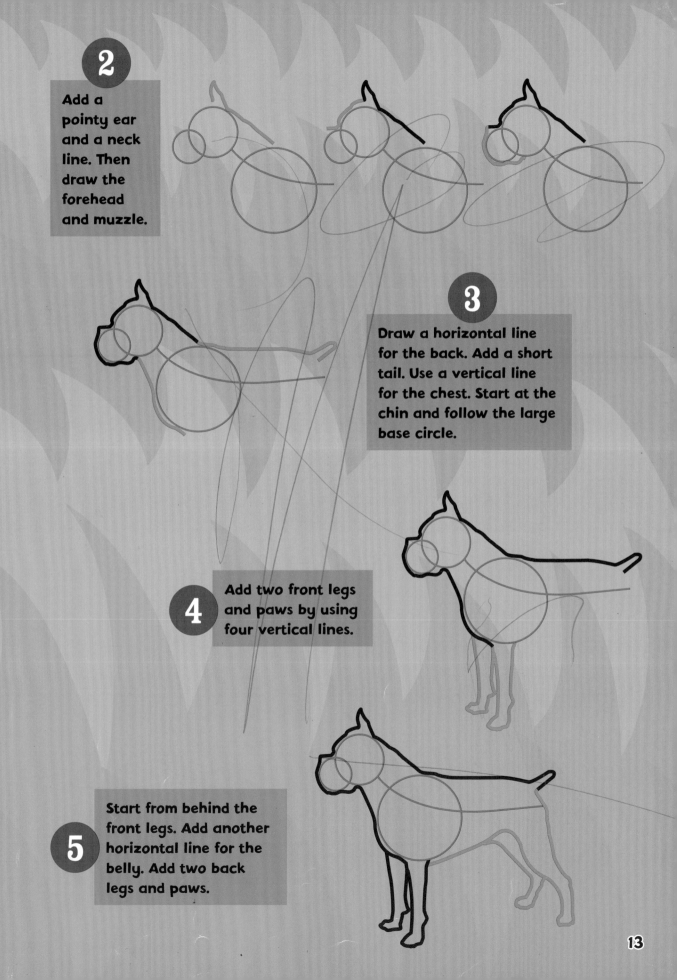

2

Add a pointy ear and a neck line. Then draw the forehead and muzzle.

3

Draw a horizontal line for the back. Add a short tail. Use a vertical line for the chest. Start at the chin and follow the large base circle.

4

Add two front legs and paws by using four vertical lines.

5

Start from behind the front legs. Add another horizontal line for the belly. Add two back legs and paws.

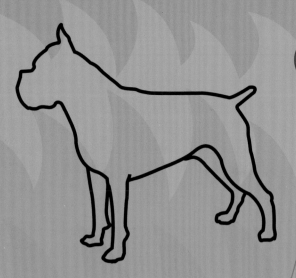

6 Carefully erase your base circles and center line.

7 Draw two circles for the eye and a half circle for the nose.

CHECK IT OUT

Many dogs wear collars with tags. Tags help owners find lost dogs.

DRAW A COLLAR WITH TAGS!

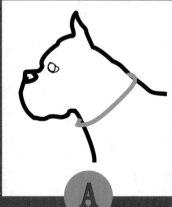

A

B

C

8 Now it is time to color your boxer!

Do you know any boxers that look like your drawing?

QUICK TIP

Mix colors to make your boxer look more realistic.

6 Carefully erase your base ovals and center line.

7 Add two small ovals above the mustache for eyes. Make two dots in the nose for nostrils. Add a small mouth line under the nose.

GET GLAM

Many owners like to dress up their Yorkies with sweaters or bows.

DRAW A FANCY BOW!

A

B

C

8 Now it is time to color your Yorkie!

TRY THIS
Color lines in the
direction the hair grows.

YORKIES are known for being fearless
watchdogs, despite their small size. Intruders beware!

HOW TO DRAW A
LABRADOR RETRIEVER

Labrador retrievers are one of the most popular breeds in the United States. Labs were bred to work with hunters. These active, athletic dogs love to swim and retrieve. Labs even have water repellent coats and webbed feet. Labs also love people and playing. Labs are smart dogs. They can be quickly trained, and they also work as therapy pets or search and rescue dogs. Labs need lots of exercise and attention to stay happy and healthy. Otherwise, they will entertain themselves by chewing and digging.

1 Make a base circle for the head. Draw a diagonal center line. Add a smaller oval overlapping the head and a larger oval for the main body shape.

2

Draw the top of the muzzle and the curve of the head. Add a U shape for the ear.

3

Make a half circle for the nose. Draw a U shape for the inside of the mouth. Add a parallel line for the jaw and a vertical line for the neck.

4

Draw a long line for the back. At the base, connect two horizontal lines for the tail. Use an S shape and a short, flat line below it for the back leg.

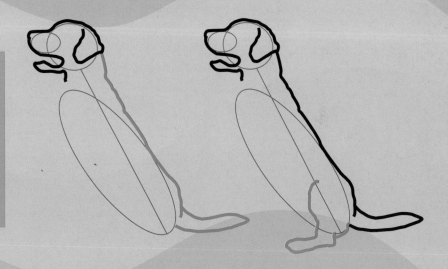

5

Draw a long, curved line for the chest from the bottom of the jaw and around the front of the oval. Use straighter, vertical lines for the two front legs.

6

Draw the rest of the belly. Add two small horizontal lines for the other back leg.

7

Before finishing the face, carefully erase your center line and base circles.

8

At the end of the muzzle, draw a small *U* for the nose. Add a teardrop shape and small circle for the eye. Draw a tongue inside the mouth and teeth along the bottom jaw.

Did you know...

Some Labs compete in hunting competitions.

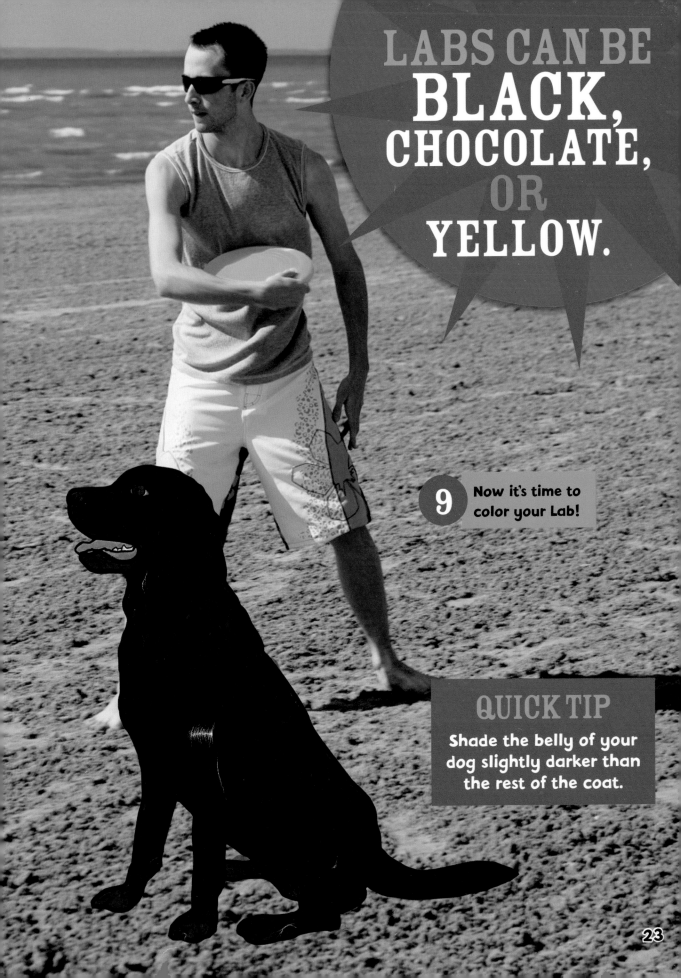

LABS CAN BE BLACK, CHOCOLATE, OR YELLOW.

9 Now it's time to color your Lab!

QUICK TIP

Shade the belly of your dog slightly darker than the rest of the coat.

HOW TO DRAW A BEAGLE

Beagles are one of the oldest breeds of hound dogs. They were brought to the United States around 1640. As a scent hound, beagles are excellent trackers. Beagles use their sense of smell to track other animals and even people. They are very curious dogs. Beagles use their adventurous nature to hunt squirrels, rabbits, and other small game. Beagles love to be part of a family, especially one that will play with them. Make sure you keep your beagle active with lots of walks and games.

1 Draw a small base circle. Add a small base rectangle to the bottom of the circle and a large base oval to the top. Draw a curved center line through the oval.

2

Outline the muzzle, the head, and the ears. Draw a large curved line for the back. Add a long, skinny tail.

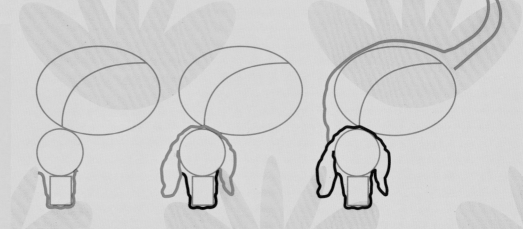

3 Add a curved back leg. Make smaller lines for the inside back leg. Use vertical lines for the front legs.

Fast Fact...

SNOOPY, CHARLIE BROWN'S DOG, WAS MODELED AFTER A BEAGLE.

4 Carefully erase your base shapes and center line.

5 Draw a large nose and two droopy eyes.

SWEET TREAT

Give your dog a bone. Rawhide bones make great chew toys.

DRAW A BONE!

A

B

C

BEAGLES are usually a mix of black and tan, with white chests.

6 Now it is time to color your beagle!

5 Carefully erase your base shapes and center line.

GOLDEN RETRIEVERS have a long, shiny coat. Their fur can be curly or wavy and is yellow, gold, red, or cream.

GOOD ADVICE

Go to a park or other spot where you can watch dogs to study how they look.

6

Draw a teardrop shape for the eyelid. For an extra challenge, try drawing a series of lines, or wrinkles, around the eye to show that your pup is sleeping.

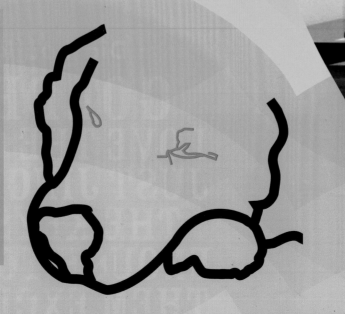

Golden retrievers love being around people.

7 Now it is time to color your golden retriever!

FURTHER READING

American Kennel Club
http://www.akc.org/kids_juniors/index.cfm?nav_area=kids_juniors

Coren, Stanley. *Why Do Dogs Have Wet Noses?* Toronto: Kids Can Press, 2008.

Dewin, Howie. *Do You Know Your Dog?: A Breed-by-Breed Guide*. New York: Scholastic, 2006.

DOGS—Caring for Your Dog
http://www.nhm.org/exhibitions/dogs/job/care.html

FBI Working Dogs
http://www.fbi.gov/kids/dogs/doghome.htm

Landau, Elaine. *Poodles Are the Best!* Minneapolis: Lerner Publications Company, 2010.

INDEX